TABLE OF CONTENTS

Understanding Web Presence 1

Building Your Foundation 7

Content is KinG 15

Search Engine Optimisation (SEO) 23

Social Media Mastery 31

Paid Advertising 41

Analytics and Performance Tracking 49

Leveraging Data for Strategy Refinement 57

Security and Compliance 67

Future Trends and Innovations 75

Case Studies and Examples 83

Conclusion and Next Steps 93

Mike Hendrikse

FOREWORD

Creating an effective web presence is, quite frankly, bloody hard. Anyone who's ever tried will tell you that. It's not just about slapping together a website and a few social media posts—it's about building something that stands out in the chaotic, fast-moving digital landscape. You need strategy, consistency, creativity, and above all, the willingness to put in the time and effort. And let's be honest, most businesses don't do this. They don't invest the resources, be it time, money, or manpower, into establishing the kind of presence that really makes a difference. The result? Missed opportunities, stagnant growth, and competitors that pull ahead.

But here's the thing—it's **doable**.

If you're willing to follow the steps, put in the work, and stay committed, you can create a web presence that doesn't just exist but thrives. This guide is designed to walk you through the essential steps to build that foundation. It's not about overloading you with technical jargon or promising overnight success. Instead, it gives you a clear, high-level understanding of what's required. You'll learn the basics, appreciate the complexity of the digital world, and hopefully, gain a strong enough grasp to know where your efforts should be focused.

Yes, this is a specialised field, and there's no sugar-coating that. You might reach a point where you need to bring in experts, or allocate more resources than you initially expected. But with this guide in hand, you'll at least have the roadmap to navigate the web marketing jungle. You'll understand what needs to be done—and more importantly, why most businesses fail to do it effectively.

The E-Volution of Business, Growing, and Sustaining Your Online Success

Copyright © 2024 by Michael Hendrikse
All rights reserved.
Published by The Online Marketer

No part of this book may be reproduced, distributed, or transmitted in any form or by any means, including photocopying, recording, or other electronic or mechanical methods, without the prior written permission of the publisher, except in the case of brief quotations embodied in critical reviews and certain other non-commercial uses permitted by copyright law.

For permission requests, please contact Mike Hendrikse at mike@theonlinemarketer.agency.

First Edition: October 2024
Cover design by Shakeel Ahmad
Edited by Mike Hendrikse

This book is a work of nonfiction. While the author has made every effort to ensure the accuracy of the information herein, the content is provided on an "as is" basis. The author and publisher disclaim any liability for errors or omissions in the content or for any potential damages arising from the use of the information in this book.

ISBN: 9798341026001

Mike Hendrikse

Dedicated to:

To Alex Venture, who encapsulates the spirit of The Online Marketer's target market. Alex represents a blend of traditional business values with a forward-thinking approach to digital marketing, embodying a typical clients journey from confusion to clarity in the online marketing landscape. We value Alex's energy and enthusiasm and her pragmatic yet visionary outlook as she commits to digital transformation.

This book won't do the work for you. But it will show you the way.

Best wishes

Mike Hendrikse

www.theonlinemarketer.agency

Mike Hendrikse

UNDERSTANDING WEB PRESENCE

THE NETWORKING EVENT

It was Alex's first networking event as the owner of her business—a small handmade jewellery company. With a portfolio of designs in hand, she walked into the bustling hall filled with potential customers, partners, and competitors. The air buzzed with conversations about business growth, new trends, and—most importantly—how to stand out online.

But as Alex made her way from booth to booth, introducing herself to fellow business owners, a pattern emerged. Every successful entrepreneur she met had one thing in common: a powerful web presence.

"I get most of my clients through my website," one said confidently.

"Oh, Instagram has been huge for our brand," said another.

Alex's stomach churned. She had no website. Sure, she had a basic Instagram page with a few posts, but it hadn't gained much traction. As she listened to more success stories, a realisation hit her—if she didn't start building an online presence, she'd be invisible in the digital world. And in today's market, being invisible was the same as being irrelevant.

Lost in thought, Alex wandered over to the coffee station, where she bumped into Jordan, a digital marketing expert with years of experience. Jordan had a calm, confident presence that immediately put Alex at ease.

"You look like someone with a lot on their mind," Jordan said with a friendly smile.

Alex sighed. "I just started a business, and it feels like everyone is talking about websites, social media, SEO… I don't even know where to begin."

"Well, that's what I help people with," Jordan replied, handing Alex his business card. "It sounds like you're thinking about your **web presence**. It's crucial in today's world, especially if you want to grow your business beyond your local community."

JORDAN'S EXPLANATION OF WEB PRESENCE

Jordan leaned against the counter, taking a sip of coffee. "Here's the thing, Alex. When we talk about 'web presence,' we're talking about how your business shows up online. It's more than just having a website—although that's a big part of it. Your web presence includes every digital touchpoint where your business can be found, from social media profiles to online reviews, even listings on directories. It's about visibility."

Alex nodded, feeling the weight of the words. "So, just having a Facebook page isn't enough?"

"Exactly. Think of your web presence as your virtual storefront. If someone searches for your jewellery online, what will they find? Is your business easy to locate? Do you look credible? Does your brand speak to who you are as a company? This is where things like SEO, social media strategy, and content come into play."

Jordan continued, "You need a cohesive online presence that's consistent across platforms. When someone searches for your brand, they should find your website, your social media profiles, maybe even interviews or features about your business. It's all about visibility and trust. If they can't find you online, it's like your business doesn't exist."

Alex bit her lip. "I get that, but how do I know if I'm doing it right?"

"That's where we'll start," Jordan said with a grin. "Let me explain why this matters first."

Why It Matters: Importance of Web Presence

Jordan pulled out his tablet, showing Alex some statistics. "Did you know that over **90% of consumers research products or services online** before making a purchase? The way you show up online can make or break your business."

They swiped to another page. "And here's something else—having a solid web presence is key to building **brand recognition**. Think about some of the brands you know and love. They all have a strong online footprint. Their websites are professional, their social media is active and engaging, and when you search for them on Google, they dominate the results. That's not by accident."

Alex looked intrigued but still a bit overwhelmed. "So, if I want people to recognise my brand, I need to be everywhere?"

"Not everywhere, but you do need to be **strategic**," Jordan clarified. "You don't need to be on every social media platform, but you need to be where your customers are.

For example, if most of your target audience is on Instagram, that's where you should focus. If they're searching for jewellery on Google, then you want to make sure your website is optimised for search engines so you show up in their results."

He paused to let Alex absorb the information before continuing.

"Another reason why your web presence matters is **customer engagement**. In today's world, your website and social media are often the first places customers interact with your brand. If your content is engaging, if your website is easy to navigate, they're more likely to trust you and eventually buy from you. But if your web presence feels disjointed, outdated, or worse—if they can't find you at all—they'll move on to your competitors."

Alex frowned. "And what about growth? I want to reach more people than just my local community."

"That's the beauty of a solid web presence," Jordan said. "It's also about **market expansion**. A well-crafted online presence allows you to expand your reach far beyond your physical location. You could be selling jewellery to someone on the other side of the world if your website, SEO, and social media strategies are aligned."

Jordan's words started to sink in. Alex could see how an online presence was no longer just an option—it was essential.

TAKEAWAY FOR READERS:

Alex's experience mirrors what many small business owners face when first confronting the importance of web presence. They realise that in today's world, having a solid web presence is the foundation of success.

Key lessons from this chapter:
1. **Web presence** is the sum of all your online touch-points — website, social media, directory listings, etc.
2. A strong web presence helps build **brand recognition** and credibility.
3. Being **strategic** about where you focus your efforts (like specific social media platforms) can yield better results than trying to be everywhere at once.

4. Your web presence is the first step in **customer engagement** and brand trust.
5. It's a key component for **market expansion**, allowing you to reach customers far beyond your local area.

As Alex leaves the networking event, her head is buzzing with ideas. She feels empowered to begin building a web presence that can help her business grow. With Jordan as her guide, she's ready to take the next step.

TRANSITION TO CHAPTER 2: BUILDING YOUR FOUNDATION

The next morning, Alex calls Jordan, determined to get started. They set up a meeting to discuss the basics of setting up a website. As Alex prepares for their first real step in the journey, she realises that the road ahead will require not just effort, but the right knowledge. The first hurdle? Figuring out what the heck a domain name and hosting plan are…

Mike Hendrikse

BUILDING YOUR FOUNDATION

THE COFFEE SHOP MEETING WITH TAYLOR

The following morning, Alex sat in her favourite local coffee shop, sipping a latte and waiting for Taylor, a web developer friend who had agreed to help. As Alex stared at her notebook filled with half-baked ideas, she felt a mixture of excitement and anxiety. She knew her business needed a website—but the technical details were intimidating.

Taylor arrived, laptop in hand, and after ordering their drinks, he sat down across from Alex.

"All right, let's build this thing," Taylor said, grinning. "But first, we've got to start with the basics—your domain and hosting."

CHOOSING THE RIGHT DOMAIN NAME

Taylor opened his laptop and typed in a domain name search tool. "So, what do you want your domain to be?"

Alex frowned. "I'm not sure… I guess just the name of my business, 'Alex's Artisan Jewellery.' But I'm worried someone already took it."

Taylor nodded. "That's a good start. Your domain name should reflect your brand, but it also needs to be **short, memorable, and easy to spell**. If the exact match for your business name isn't available, we can try slight variations."

They typed 'alexsartisanjewellery.com' into the search bar, and as predicted, it was already taken.

"No worries," Taylor said. "We can try different options. Maybe 'alexjewellerydesigns.com' or 'artisanjewellerybyalex.com.'"

Alex jotted down the suggestions, starting to see how flexibility was necessary. "What about things like .com versus .co.za, .net or .shop?"

"Good question. The '.com' domain is still the most widely recognised and trusted, but depending on your brand, alternative domain extensions like '.shop' could work, especially since you're in retail or geographically bound. Just make sure it's easy for people to remember and doesn't sound overly complicated."

Taylor paused, then added, "And don't forget to check if the domain matches your social media handles. You want consistency across platforms."

UNDERSTANDING HOSTING OPTIONS

Once they settled on a few potential domain names, Taylor moved on to the next step: hosting. "Now that you've got an idea for your domain, let's talk about hosting. Basically, your website needs a home on the internet, and that's what web hosting provides."

Alex looked puzzled. "Can't I just put my website online without paying for hosting?"

Taylor chuckled. "I wish it worked that way. Think of your domain as your street address, and hosting as the plot of land where your house—the website—actually sits. Without hosting, your website has nowhere to live."

Alex's eyes widened in realisation. "Okay, so how do I choose the right hosting?"

"There are different types of hosting depending on your needs," Taylor explained, pulling up a comparison chart. "If you're just starting out, a **shared hosting plan** is affordable and works for small websites, but you're sharing server space with other sites, which can slow things down. For higher traffic and better performance, you might want to consider **VPS hosting** or **dedicated hosting**, but those come at a higher price."

Alex scribbled notes. "I don't think I'll need high traffic hosting right away, so shared hosting sounds good to start."

"Exactly," Taylor said, nodding in approval. "And later on, if your business grows, you can always upgrade your hosting plan."

WEBSITE DESIGN: PRINCIPLES OF USER-FRIENDLY DESIGN

With the basics of domain and hosting covered, Taylor leaned back in their chair and smiled. "Now comes the fun part— designing the website."

Alex's excitement dimmed a little. "Fun? It feels overwhelming. I don't know anything about web design."

"Don't worry. I've got you," Taylor reassured. "The key thing to remember is that **user-friendly design** is everything. A beautiful website doesn't mean much if it's hard to use. You want to make sure that visitors can navigate it easily and find what they're looking for. That's what keeps them engaged."

Taylor began to sketch out a basic site map on a napkin, labelling it: **Home, About Us, Products, Blog, Contact.**

"See? Simple is better. Your homepage should be clean and tell visitors exactly what you offer—no clutter. And make sure there's a clear call to action—something that tells visitors what to do next, like 'Shop Now' or 'Subscribe.'"

They emphasised a few other essentials:
- **Intuitive navigation**: Use clear, simple menus so users can easily explore the site.

- **Consistent branding**: "Your logo, colours, and fonts should all match your brand identity."
- **Contact details**: "Make it easy for customers to reach you—whether that's a contact form, email, or phone number."
- **Accessibility**: "Make sure your website is easy to read and navigate for everyone, including people with disabilities."

Alex was starting to feel more confident. "Okay, so I don't need anything too fancy—just something clean and functional."

"Exactly," Taylor said. "And speaking of functionality…"

Mobile Optimisation: The Importance of Responsive Design

Taylor opened a few websites on their phone, showing Alex how some websites looked great on a desktop but awful on mobile. "Most of web traffic comes from mobile devices. If your website isn't optimised for phones and tablets, you're missing out on a huge chunk of potential customers."

Alex frowned, recalling their own frustration with clunky mobile websites. "So how do I make sure it works on all devices?"

"That's called **responsive design**. It means your website automatically adjusts to different screen sizes. Most modern website builders like WordPress or Shopify have responsive templates built-in, so you don't have to worry about coding it yourself."

They scrolled through a few website templates, showing how the layout changed depending on whether it was viewed on a phone, tablet, or desktop.

"You want images to resize properly, text to be readable without zooming in, and buttons big enough for thumbs to tap easily," Taylor explained. "Think about the user experience. If it's frustrating to navigate, they'll leave."

Branding Consistency

Taylor then pulled up an example of a website that had a confusing mix of fonts, colours, and messaging. "Now, let's talk about **branding consistency**."

Alex raised an eyebrow. "Branding? Isn't that just about having a logo?"

"Not quite," Taylor said. "Branding is about creating a cohesive identity that customers recognise and trust. It's not just your logo —it's your colour scheme, the tone of your copy, the fonts you use. Everything should work together to tell your brand's story."

They pulled up Alex's Instagram page and asked, "What's your brand's personality?"

Alex thought for a moment. "It's handmade, so it should feel personal, maybe a little earthy and artisanal, but still elegant."

"Great," Taylor said, typing away. "Now let's make sure that vibe carries across everything—your website, your social media, your emails. The goal is that anywhere someone sees you online, they know it's your brand."

The Highlights: Responsive Design, Speed, and User Experience

As their coffee cups emptied, Taylor summarised the key points for Alex to remember:

- **Responsive design**: Your website needs to look great on all devices, from desktops to mobile phones.
- **Speed**: A slow-loading site will drive users away. Use optimised images, avoid heavy plugins, and choose fast hosting.

- **User experience**: Always design with your customer in mind. Is the site easy to navigate? Can they find what they need? Does it feel professional and trustworthy?

Alex left the coffee shop feeling energised. The idea of building a website no longer felt so intimidating. They now had a clear understanding of what was needed—a memorable domain name, reliable hosting, and a website that was simple, clean, and optimised for both desktop and mobile users.

TAKEAWAY FOR READERS

Just like Alex, many new business owners struggle with the technical aspects of creating a website. The key lessons from this chapter are:

1. **Domain and Hosting**: Your domain is your digital address; choose one that's memorable and consistent with your brand. Hosting is where your website lives—start small with shared hosting, and scale as your business grows. The Online marketer offers such hosting services.
2. **User-Friendly Design**: Simple, intuitive navigation is more important than flashy design. Make sure your website is clean, easy to use, and focused on guiding visitors toward a clear call to action.
3. **Mobile Optimisation**: With so much traffic coming from mobile, your website must be responsive. Use templates that automatically adjust for different devices.
4. **Branding Consistency**: Ensure your website reflects your brand identity through colours, fonts, tone, and messaging, creating a cohesive experience across all platforms.

5. **Speed and Experience**: A slow site or poor user experience can drive customers away, so prioritise speed and usability.

TRANSITION TO CHAPTER 3: CONTENT IS KING

Armed with a domain, hosting, and a web design plan, Alex is ready to take the next step—filling her site with content. But what kind of content should they create? As they begin brainstorming blog posts, videos, and product descriptions, she quickly realises that this next stage of building a web presence will require a whole new strategy.

Enter Jordan again, with advice on why **content is king**…

Mike Hendrikse

CONTENT IS KING

ALEX'S WORKSHOP MEETING WITH JORDAN

A few days after their coffee shop meeting with Taylor, Alex found herself in the midst of another challenge. Her website was nearly ready, but it felt... empty. Sure, it looked clean and professional, but without content, it was like a shop with no products on the shelves. So Alex called Jordan again for help, asking him to swing by her workshop to discuss how to create meaningful content for the site.

Jordan arrived just as Alex was sorting through some materials for her latest collection. The workshop was filled with tools, gemstones, and half-finished pieces of jewellery—Alex's creativity was in full bloom, but that didn't seem to translate into the online space.

"You've built a great foundation," Jordan said, gesturing to the computer where the homepage was displayed. "Now it's time to fill it with content that tells your story, engages your audience, and brings traffic to your site. In other words, we need to build your **content strategy**."

CONTENT STRATEGY: DEVELOPING A PLAN

Alex looked at Jordan, confused. "I keep hearing that 'content is king,' but I'm not sure what that means exactly. I'm a jewellery designer, not a writer."

Jordan smiled. "Content isn't just about writing blog posts. It's about providing value. It's anything that informs, entertains, or engages your audience, whether that's through articles, videos, social media posts, or even product descriptions. The key is to <u>develop a strategy</u> that aligns with your business goals."

Jordan pulled out a whiteboard and began sketching a simple content plan. "Here's how I think about it. Every piece of content should fit into one of these categories:

1. **Educational content** – teaching your audience something valuable (e.g., 'How to Care for Handmade Jewellery' or 'The History Behind Birthstones').
2. **Inspirational content** – stories, testimonials, or behind-the-scenes content that connects emotionally with your audience.
3. **Promotional content** – showcasing your products, upcoming sales, or exclusive offers.
4. **Entertaining content** – things that are fun and engaging, like behind-the-scenes videos, humour, or collaborations with influencers."

Alex nodded slowly, starting to get it. "So it's not just about selling?"

"Exactly!" Jordan replied. "In fact, the best content isn't a sales pitch at all. It's about building trust and creating relationships. When people find your content helpful or inspiring, they're more likely to come back to your site—and eventually, they'll buy."

Quality Over Quantity: The Value of High-Impact Content

As they talked, Alex began to feel overwhelmed by the sheer amount of content she thought they needed to produce. "But I don't have time to write a new blog post every day or shoot videos every week."

Jordan shook his head. "You don't need to churn out content just for the sake of having more. The goal is **quality over quantity**. It's much better to post one high-value piece of content a week than five mediocre posts."

Jordan grabbed a piece of paper and wrote down a few pointers:

- **Solve a problem**: Think about the questions your customers are asking. If you answer those questions with your content, it's immediately valuable to them.
- **Be original**: Your customers want to hear from *you*—your insights, your experiences, your voice. Don't just copy what your competitors are doing.
- **Create evergreen content**: Focus on topics that will still be relevant months or even years from now, like a guide on choosing the perfect engagement ring or how to layer jewellery.

Jordan emphasised, "The goal is to create content that resonates with your audience and positions you as an authority in your niche. When people see you as a trusted source, they'll come to you when they're ready to buy."

Content Pillars and the Editorial Calendar

"Okay, but how do I actually organise all of this?" Alex asked, jotting down notes frantically. "It feels like there's so much I could talk about—where do I start?"

Jordan grinned, clearly excited to explain the next part. "That's where **content pillars** come in. Think of these as the core topics that your brand focuses on. Since you're in the jewellery business, your content pillars might be things like:

- Jewellery care and maintenance
- Fashion and style tips

- Behind-the-scenes of your creative process
- Special occasions and gift guides

"These pillars act as the foundation for all your content," Jordan continued. "Once you've defined them, it's much easier to plan out what you'll create."

Alex felt a bit of relief. This made sense—focusing on a few main themes would make content creation more manageable.

"To keep it all organised, you'll want an **editorial calendar**," Jordan said, pulling up a template. "This helps you plan ahead and stay consistent. Let's say you post one blog a week. You could rotate between your content pillars—one week it's a jewellery care guide, the next week a style tip, and so on."

Alex was already picturing the calendar on their wall, mapping out blog posts, videos, and social media updates over the next few months.

SEO-Friendly Content: Keywords and Structure

As they brainstormed topics, Alex asked, "How does this help people actually find my site? What's the connection between content and SEO?"

Jordan sat up, ready to dive into the next crucial topic.

"That's a great question. The content you create needs to be SEO-friendly. This means that it includes the keywords people are searching for when they look for products or information related to your business."

They pulled up Google and typed "handmade jewellery care tips." Immediately, dozens of search results popped up.

"See these top results? They're showing up here because they've optimised their content with keywords that match what people are searching for. You'll want to do the same.

Research **keywords** that are relevant to your business—tools like Google Keyword Planner or Ubersuggest can help. Then, naturally integrate those keywords into your content."

Jordan scribbled down a quick outline for Alex:
- Use the **main keyword** in the title and introduction.
- Break content into sections with **subheadings** (search engines love organised content).
- Include relevant keywords in meta descriptions, image alt text, and even in your URLs.

"And remember," Jordan added, "good SEO isn't just about keywords. It's also about **quality and structure**. Search engines reward sites that offer valuable, well-organised information. So, if your blog posts are useful and easy to read, you'll rank higher in search results."

Repurposing Content: Maximise Your Efforts

By this point, Alex's head was buzzing with ideas, but she still looked a little overwhelmed. "This is all great, but I'm worried about keeping up with everything. It seems like a lot of work."

Jordan smiled knowingly. "That's where **content repurposing** comes in. You don't always need to create new content from scratch. Think about how you can take one piece of content and repurpose it across different platforms."

Jordan explained with an example: "Let's say you write a blog post about 'The Top 5 Jewellery Trends for 2024.' You could:
- Turn each trend into an individual Instagram post, with a beautiful image of your jewellery that fits the trend.
- Create a video for TikTok or YouTube, explaining how to style those pieces.
- Take one trend and expand it into a longer post or video.

- Use snippets from the blog for an email newsletter to your subscribers."

Alex's eyes lit up. "So I'm not starting from scratch every time?"

"Exactly," Jordan said. "Work smarter, not harder. Repurposing helps you get more mileage out of every piece of content."

The Highlights: Content Pillars, SEO, and Consistency

As their conversation wrapped up, Jordan summarised the key points Alex needed to remember:

1. **Content strategy** is the <u>blueprint for all the content</u> you create. It should be driven by your business goals and your audience's needs.
2. Focus on **quality over quantity**. It's better to post one high-value blog a week than multiple rushed pieces.
3. Use **content pillars** to guide your topics. These are the core areas of expertise that you want to be known for.
4. **SEO-friendly content** ensures that your audience can find you. Research keywords and integrate them naturally into your posts.
5. **Repurpose content** across different platforms to maximise its impact and save time.

TAKEAWAY FOR READERS:

Much like Alex, many entrepreneurs feel overwhelmed by the prospect of content creation. The key lessons from this chapter are:

1. **Content is about value**, not volume. Think about what will genuinely help, inform, or entertain your audience.

2. Develop a clear **content strategy** that aligns with your business goals and focuses on core topics (content pillars).
3. Create **SEO-friendly content** by researching relevant keywords and ensuring your content is structured for search engines.
4. **Consistency** is more important than frequency. Stick to a schedule that works for you, and use an editorial calendar to stay organised.
5. **Repurpose content** to get the most out of your efforts. One blog post can fuel multiple social media updates, videos, and newsletters.

TRANSITION TO CHAPTER 4: SEARCH ENGINE OPTIMISATION (SEO)

With a solid content strategy in place, Alex felt more confident about creating value for her customers. But there was one more hurdle—how to get her content in front of the right people. It was time to dive deeper into **SEO**. As Alex and Jordan met once again

Mike Hendrikse

SEARCH ENGINE OPTIMISATION (SEO)

A MEETING WITH JORDAN ON SEO BASICS

A week after launching her first batch of blog posts, Alex sat down with Jordan again—this time at her workshop. The website was live, the content was flowing, but Alex still wasn't seeing much traffic. Despite her new blog and polished Instagram posts, the silence was deafening. Frustrated, Alex asked Jordan for help once more.

Jordan arrived with his usual energy, but this time armed with a folder of charts, keyword lists, and tools. As they sat down in front of Alex's computer, Jordan broke the silence. "It's time we talked about **SEO**."

Alex's brow furrowed. "I thought I was already doing SEO—using keywords and everything."

"You've got the basics," Jordan replied, pulling up the website on the screen. "But SEO is like building a reputation. It takes time, effort, and a solid strategy. It's not just about having keywords—it's about using them effectively, and that's just the beginning. Let's break it down."

SEO Basics: Keywords, Meta Tags, and Backlinks

Jordan began with a blank document, writing "SEO" in big letters across the top. "At its core, **Search Engine Optimisation (SEO)** is the process of improving your website so that search engines like Google can understand it and rank it higher in search results. The higher you rank, the more people will find you."

Alex nodded, eager to understand more. "So, it's not just about having a website, but making sure Google can find it?"

"Exactly," Jordan confirmed. "There are three key factors that play a big role in SEO: **keywords**, **meta tags**, and **backlinks**."

1. Keywords: The Foundation of SEO

Jordan pulled up one of Alex's blog posts about jewellery care. "This is great content, but the problem is that you're using the wrong keywords. You need to think about what your customers are actually typing into Google when they search for information."

Jordan introduced Alex to tools like **Google Keyword Planner** and **Ubersuggest** to find relevant search terms. They typed in "handmade jewellery care," and dozens of keyword suggestions appeared.

"Look at these," Jordan said, pointing to the list. "You'll see terms like 'how to clean handmade jewellery' and 'caring for silver jewellery.' These are long-tail keywords—specific phrases that your customers are searching for. You need to use these in your blog post titles, headings, and throughout your content."

Jordan listed some practical tips:
- **Keyword placement**: Use your target keyword in the title, the first 100 words, and in at least one subheading. Sprinkle it naturally throughout the content but don't overdo it.
- **LSI keywords**: Use related keywords (known as Latent Semantic Indexing keywords) to make your content more relevant. These are words or phrases that are semantically linked to your primary keyword.

- **Keyword research tools**: Always use tools like Google Keyword Planner or Ahrefs to check what keywords are being searched the most.

2. Meta Tags: Your Website's Secret Weapon

Jordan clicked over to Alex's homepage and opened the HTML code. "Let's talk about **meta tags**. These are small snippets of code that describe your page's content to search engines."

Alex looked puzzled as Jordan explained. "There are two key meta tags you need to know about: the **meta title** and the **meta description**. These don't show up on your website, but they do show up in search engine results."

Jordan pulled up a sample search result from Google. "See this?" They pointed to the clickable headline. "That's the meta title. And this," they pointed to the short description below the headline, "is the meta description."

Jordan explained how important it was to craft these carefully:

- **Meta title**: This should be a concise, keyword-rich title that describes your page's content. Keep it under 60 characters so it doesn't get cut off.
- **Meta description**: This is your chance to convince searchers to click on your link. It should be no more than 160 characters and include your main keyword, plus a call to action.

"For example," Jordan said, "if you're writing about jewellery care, your meta title might be 'How to Clean and Care for Handmade Jewellery | Alex's Artisan Jewellery.' The meta description could be something like 'Learn the best techniques to clean and protect your handmade jewellery. Expert tips from Alex's Artisan Jewellery.'"

3. Backlinks: Building Authority

Next, Jordan explained the concept of **backlinks**. "Think of backlinks as votes of confidence. When other websites link to your content, it tells search engines that your site is credible and valuable."

Alex's eyes widened. "So, I need other websites to link to me?"

"Exactly," Jordan confirmed. "The more high-quality sites that link to you, the more Google trusts your content. But not all backlinks are created equal. Links from authoritative sites—like industry blogs, news outlets, or reputable businesses—are far more valuable than random or low-quality links."

"How do I get these backlinks?" Alex asked, feeling a bit daunted.

"There are a few strategies," Jordan said, jotting down notes:

- **Guest posting**: Write articles for other blogs or websites in exchange for a link back to your site.
- **Influencer outreach**: Connect with influencers or bloggers in the jewellery or fashion space who might want to feature your products or mention your blog posts.
- **Content promotion**: Share your blog posts and videos on social media, in online communities, and with industry professionals. The more visibility you have, the more likely others are to link to your content.

On-Page vs. Off-Page SEO: Techniques for Both Types

With the basics covered, Jordan moved on to explain the difference between **on-page** and **off-page SEO**.

"**On-page SEO** is everything you can control on your website," Jordan explained. "That includes things like:

- **Keyword optimisation** (using keywords in your content, meta tags, and URLs).
- **Content structure** (using headings, bullet points, and short paragraphs to make your content easy to read).
- **Internal linking** (linking to other relevant pages on your own site). This helps both users and search engines navigate your content.
- **Image optimisation** (using descriptive alt text for images). This not only improves accessibility but also helps with SEO."

Alex leaned forward. "And what about off-page SEO?"

"**Off-page SEO** is everything that happens off your website that impacts your rankings—primarily backlinks, social media shares, and online mentions. It's about building your website's authority in the eyes of search engines."

SEO Tools: Keyword Research, SEO Audits, and More

Jordan pulled up a few tools to show Alex how to manage their SEO efforts. "There are tons of tools that can help you with SEO," Jordan said. "Here are a few you should know about."

1. **Google Search Console**: "This free tool from Google helps you monitor your site's performance in search results. You can see what keywords are driving traffic and where you need to improve."
2. **Rank Math SEO (for WordPress)**: "If you're using WordPress, RankMath SEO is a plugin that helps you optimise every page and blog post for SEO. It'll guide you through setting up meta tags, keyword density, and readability."

3. **SEMrush or Ahrefs**: "These are premium tools that give you deep insights into your site's SEO performance. You can track backlinks, conduct keyword research, and even audit your site for SEO issues."

Alex jotted down the names of the tools, feeling a bit more equipped. "This makes it feel more manageable," she said.

THE HIGHLIGHTS: SEO STRATEGY ESSENTIALS

Jordan summed up the session with a few key takeaways:
1. **Keywords**: Research long-tail keywords that your customers are searching for. Use them strategically in your titles, headings, and throughout your content.
2. **Meta tags**: Optimise your meta titles and descriptions to improve click-through rates in search results.
3. **Backlinks**: Build credibility by earning backlinks from reputable websites. Quality matters more than quantity.
4. **On-page SEO**: Ensure your site is easy to navigate, content is well-structured, and images are optimised.
5. **Off-page SEO**: Promote your content, build relationships, and aim to increase your site's authority through backlinks and mentions.

TAKEAWAY FOR READERS:

For business owners like Alex, SEO can seem complex and overwhelming, but it's a crucial part of building a successful web presence. The key lessons from this chapter are:

1. **SEO is a long game**: It takes time to see results, but a well-executed strategy can dramatically improve your website's visibility.
2. **Keywords**: Start with keyword research to find out what your audience is searching for. Focus on long-tail keywords that are specific and easier to rank for.
3. **On-page SEO**: Optimise your site's content, structure, and meta tags to make it easy for search engines to understand and rank your pages.
4. **Off-page SEO**: Build authority by earning backlinks from high-quality websites and promoting your content through social media and outreach.
5. **Tools**: Use tools like Google Search Console, RankMath SEO, and SEMrush to monitor and improve your SEO performance.

TRANSITION TO CHAPTER 5: SOCIAL MEDIA MASTERY

As Alex started to grasp the fundamentals of SEO, she realised that search engine traffic was only part of the equation. To truly build her brand, she needed to engage with her audience on social media. In the next chapter, Jordan would guide Alex through the world of **social media mastery**, helping her to choose the right platforms and create content that resonates with her audience…

SOCIAL MEDIA MASTERY

A SOCIAL MEDIA STRATEGY SESSION

After diving into the world of SEO, Alex had another pressing challenge—social media. The thought of managing multiple social platforms felt overwhelming, especially given the constant demands for updates, engagement, and fresh content. One afternoon, she called Jordan to brainstorm how to master this part of the business.

They met at Alex's workshop, the familiar clink and hiss of jewellery making tools in the background as Jordan arrived, carrying his tablet. As they settled into the discussion, Jordan opened by saying, "Social media isn't just about posting regularly. It's about being **strategic**—understanding where your audience is, what they want, and how to connect with them in meaningful ways."

Alex nodded, a bit anxious but eager to learn. "So, where do I even start? There are so many platforms, and I feel like I can't keep up."

Jordan smiled knowingly. "That's the first trap a lot of businesses fall into. You don't need to be on every platform—you just need to be on the ones that matter to your audience."

CHOOSING THE RIGHT PLATFORMS: WHERE IS YOUR AUDIENCE?

Jordan pulled up a list of popular social media platforms: Instagram, Facebook, TikTok, Pinterest, LinkedIn, and X (previously known as Twitter). Each had its own strengths and audience, and Jordan knew Alex's business wouldn't need all of them.

"You're a jewellery brand, right?" Jordan began. "Think about where your customers are most likely to spend their time. For a visual, creative business like yours, platforms like **Instagram**, **Pinterest**, and maybe even **TikTok** are ideal."

Alex raised an eyebrow at TikTok. "I get Instagram and Pinterest, but why TikTok? Isn't that mostly for teenagers?"

"Not anymore," Jordan explained. "TikTok has a rapidly growing user base of adults, especially in the creative and fashion spaces. If you can create engaging, short-form videos showing the process behind your designs or how to style your pieces, it could be a goldmine for your brand."

Jordan then broke down each platform:

- **Instagram**: Perfect for showcasing the beauty and craftsmanship of your jewellery. Use the feed for high-quality photos and the stories for behind-the-scenes glimpses into your process. Don't forget about Instagram shopping and the use of hashtags for discoverability.

- **Pinterest**: This is a great platform for **discovery**. People go on Pinterest to find inspiration, especially for things like fashion, weddings, and gifts. Pin your products, style ideas, and jewellery care tips to reach users who are actively looking for ideas and products like yours.

- **TikTok**: Ideal for engaging, creative content. You can show your audience the design process, how to wear certain pieces, or even do fun challenges related to fashion and jewellery. TikTok's algorithm is also great for exposing your content to a broad audience.

- **Facebook**: While not as visually driven as Instagram or Pinterest, Facebook still has its uses, especially for ads and creating a business page that acts as a secondary website where customers can find reviews, shop updates, and engage with your community.

Jordan emphasised, "You don't need to dominate all these platforms. Pick two or three and focus your energy on creating high-quality, engaging content for them."

Content for Social Media: Tailoring to Each Platform

Once Alex had a sense of which platforms to focus on, her next question was, "What kind of content works best for each?"

Jordan smiled. "Each platform has its own style and audience expectations. Here's a breakdown of what works best."

Instagram

- **Visual storytelling** is key. Post high-quality images of your products, but also include lifestyle photos that show your jewellery in action.
- **Stories**: Use Instagram Stories to showcase daily updates, flash sales, or behind-the-scenes content. Polls, quizzes, and countdowns create engagement.
- **Reels**: Short, engaging videos are increasingly important on Instagram. Show how to style your jewellery, share design tips, or give a quick look at how your pieces are made.

Pinterest

- **Pins**: Create attractive, vertical images that link back to your website or product pages. Think about seasonal content—gift guides, jewellery trends, or styling tips for specific occasions like weddings or holidays.
- **Boards**: Curate boards around themes your audience loves, such as "Boho Jewellery for Summer" or "Gifts for Her." This drives more discovery and repins.

TikTok

- **Behind-the-scenes videos**: Show the making of your jewellery or the craftsmanship involved in each piece.
- **Styling tips**: Quick videos on how to wear or layer your pieces.
- **Trending challenges**: Participate in relevant TikTok challenges that align with your brand's style or personality.

Facebook

- **Posts**: Focus on sharing blog posts, product updates, and customer testimonials. Facebook is less about daily visuals and more about community engagement and updates.
- **Groups**: Consider starting a Facebook group where your customers can interact with you, share how they style your jewellery, or offer feedback on upcoming designs.

Jordan leaned in, adding, "Always think about your audience. What do they care about? What kind of content would they find useful, entertaining, or inspiring? That's how you build **engagement**."

SOCIAL MEDIA ADVERTISING: GETTING STARTED WITH PAID SOCIAL

As they discussed content, Alex's mind began to wander to the question of advertising. "What about paid ads? Is it worth investing in?"

Jordan nodded thoughtfully. "Absolutely, but like everything else, it has to be done strategically. The good news is that platforms like Instagram and Facebook allow for highly **targeted ads**."

They opened a dashboard to walk Alex through the basics of **social media advertising**:

1. **Define your goal**: Do you want more followers? Website traffic? Sales? Your ads need a clear objective. For example, if you're launching a new jewellery collection, your goal might be direct purchases, while a giveaway might aim to grow your email list or follower count.

2. **Target the right audience**: Social platforms have incredible targeting options. You can set parameters based on location, age, interests, and even behaviour. For example, target people who have shown interest in fashion, jewellery, or handmade goods.

3. Ad formats:
   - **Carousel ads**: Show multiple images or videos in a single ad. Great for highlighting a collection.
   - **Video ads**: Short videos that demonstrate the beauty or functionality of your products.
   - **Story ads**: Full-screen ads that appear in Instagram and Facebook Stories. These are highly engaging, especially for limited-time offers.

4. **Budgeting**: Start small, Jordan advised, maybe with a budget of $5-10 per day to test the waters. "Once you see what works, you can scale up," Jordan explained. "The key is to monitor your ads regularly and adjust based on performance."

5. **Tracking performance**: Use **Facebook Ads Manager** or **Instagram Insights** to track how your ads are doing. Metrics like **click-through rates**, **conversion rates**, and **cost-per-click** will help you refine your strategy.

Jordan encouraged Alex to experiment with small campaigns. "Run A/B tests—try different visuals, headlines, or offers to see what resonates best with your audience. Paid social can be powerful if you keep tweaking it."

Engagement Strategies: Building a Community

Alex's next concern was how to actually get people to interact with their posts. "I post sometimes, but it feels like no one's really engaging. What am I doing wrong?"

Jordan leaned forward, ready to explain the art of social media engagement. "Social media isn't just a one-way street where you post and leave. It's about building relationships. **Engagement** is what fuels the algorithms, so the more people like, comment, and share your posts, the more visibility you get."

He offered a few proven strategies:
- **Ask questions**: Encourage followers to engage by asking questions in your captions. For example, "Which of these new designs do you like best?" or "What's your favourite way to style layered necklaces?"

- **Polls and interactive features**: Use Instagram's poll or quiz features to create fun, quick engagements. It could be something as simple as asking, "Silver or gold?" for preferences on your new collection.
- **User-generated content (UGC)**: Encourage your customers to share photos of them wearing your jewellery and tag your brand. Feature these posts on your page as testimonials or in your stories.
- **Respond to comments**: When people comment on your posts, respond to them! A quick reply or even a 'like' lets them know you're paying attention. It builds loyalty and encourages future engagement.
- **Contests and giveaways**: Run occasional giveaways to boost engagement. Ask people to like, comment, and share your post to enter. Giveaways are a powerful way to attract new followers and increase visibility.

Social Listening: Tuning into Conversations About Your Brand

Jordan introduced one more advanced concept: **social listening**. "This is about tracking conversations online—not just the ones directly involving you, but the ones relevant to your industry or audience."

They explained how Alex could use tools like **Hootsuite** or **Sprout Social** to monitor social media for mentions of their brand, competitors, or specific keywords like "handmade jewellery" or "custom rings."

"Social listening lets you see what people are saying about your niche and helps you spot trends early. It can also help you engage with potential customers who haven't even heard of you yet. For example, if someone tweets, 'Looking for handmade jewellery for my wedding,' you can jump in and offer a suggestion."

The Highlights: Engagement, Ads, and Strategy

As their session wound down, Jordan summarised the most important takeaways for Alex:
1. **Choose platforms wisely**: Focus on two or three social media platforms where your target audience spends their time. Don't spread yourself too thin.
2. **Tailor your content**: Each platform has its own style. Use Instagram for beautiful visuals, Pinterest for discovery, TikTok for short, engaging videos, and Facebook for building community and running ads.
3. **Paid ads**: Social media advertising can drive traffic and sales when done strategically. Start small, experiment, and target the right audience.
4. **Engagement is key**: Ask questions, use interactive features, respond to comments, and encourage user-generated content. Engagement boosts your visibility.
5. **Social listening**: Stay in tune with online conversations about your brand and industry. Use these insights to create content and engage with your audience.

TAKEAWAY FOR READERS:

Like Alex, many small business owners struggle to harness the power of social media. The key lessons from this chapter are:
1. **Strategic platform selection**: Focus on the platforms where your audience is most active, whether that's Instagram, Pinterest, or TikTok.

2. **Tailored content**: Create content that fits the style of each platform, from visually stunning photos on Instagram to engaging, short videos on TikTok.
3. **Paid social ads**: Use social media advertising strategically, targeting your audience with clear goals and small budgets to start.
4. **Engagement**: Build a loyal community by encouraging interaction through questions, polls, and user-generated content.
5. **Social listening**: Monitor conversations relevant to your brand and industry to stay ahead of trends and engage with potential customers.

TRANSITION TO CHAPTER 6: PAID ADVERTISING

With their social media strategy now taking shape, Alex began to wonder about more traditional forms of online advertising—specifically **pay-per-click (PPC)** campaigns. In the next chapter, Alex and Jordan dive into the world of **paid advertising**, learning how to set up effective PPC campaigns, track results, and use retargeting to bring back potential customers who didn't make a purchase the first time…

Mike Hendrikse

PAID ADVERTISING

ALEX'S FIRST DIVE INTO PAID ADVERTISING

After weeks of refining their social media strategy, Alex had finally started seeing some traction. Her Instagram following was slowly growing, and Pinterest was driving visitors to the site. But despite all the engagement, actual sales were still trickling in slower than expected. Frustration was setting in. It was then that Alex decided it was time to explore **paid advertising**—something she'd been avoiding, assuming it was too complex or expensive.

Naturally, Alex reached out to Jordan once again. They met at a local café, and Alex wasted no time diving in. "I think I need to start running ads. Organic traffic is great, but I feel like I'm not reaching enough people. How do I start?"

Jordan smiled. "You're right, paid advertising can be a game-changer—if you do it strategically. Let's talk about **PPC**, retargeting, and how to make sure you're not throwing money away."

Introduction to PPC: Pay-Per-Click Advertising Explained

Jordan opened his laptop, pulling up an example of a Google search results page. "Let's start with the basics. PPC—**Pay-Per-Click advertising**—is exactly what it sounds like. You only pay when someone clicks on your ad. You can run PPC campaigns on platforms like **Google Ads**, **Facebook**, and **Instagram**."

They clicked on a search ad at the top of the results. "See this? It's a Google ad. You bid on keywords so that your ad shows up when people search for terms related to your business. Every time someone clicks on this ad, the advertiser pays a fee."

Alex scribbled notes, already feeling the weight of the jargon. "So, I'm bidding against other people for these keywords?"

"Exactly," Jordan confirmed. "But here's the thing—you're not just bidding on price. Google also looks at the **quality of your ad** and the **relevance** of your landing page. If your ad is well-written and your landing page matches the search intent, you can actually outbid competitors who are paying more per click."

Choosing Keywords for PPC Campaigns

Jordan took Alex through the first critical step of setting up a PPC campaign: **choosing the right keywords**.

"Let's go back to your jewellery business," Jordan said. "Think about what your potential customers are searching for. It might be something specific like 'handmade gold necklaces' or 'custom wedding rings.' You'll want to use tools like **Google Keyword Planner** or **SEMrush** to figure out what keywords have high search volumes and low competition."

Jordan typed in a few keywords related to handmade jewellery into Google Keyword Planner. "See this? 'Custom gold earrings' has a lower cost per click than 'handmade jewellery,' but it's still highly relevant to what you sell. You want to target specific, long-tail keywords like this because they're less competitive and more likely to convert."

Alex nodded. "So, how do I balance keywords that are popular but also affordable?"

"Great question. The goal is to find a **sweet spot** where the keywords are relevant to your product, aren't too expensive, and have a decent search volume. That way, you're not paying a fortune for clicks, but you're still targeting people who are looking for exactly what you offer."

Setting Up Your First Google Ads Campaign

Jordan guided Alex through the step-by-step process of setting up their first **Google Ads** campaign.

1. **Choose your campaign type**: Jordan explained the different types of ads available—**search ads** (which appear in Google search results), **display ads** (which appear on websites in Google's ad network), and **shopping ads** (which show images of products directly in search results). For Alex, a **search ad campaign** was the best place to start.

2. **Create your ad copy**: Jordan pulled up an example of a well-written ad. "Your ad needs to be compelling and clear. Include your keyword in the headline, emphasise a benefit, and have a strong **call-to-action (CTA)**. For example: 'Handmade Gold Necklaces – Free Shipping & Custom Designs.'"

3. **Set a budget**: Jordan recommended starting with a **daily budget** of $5-10. "Google Ads lets you set a budget that you're comfortable with. You can always increase it later once you start seeing results."

4. **Target your audience**: Alex had the option to target their ads geographically, which Jordan advised to use wisely. "If you offer international shipping, you can target globally, but if you're focused on local sales, you can set your ads to

show only to people in certain areas."

5. **Monitor and optimise**: Once the campaign is live, Alex could track metrics like **click-through rate (CTR)** and **conversion rate**. "You'll need to monitor your campaigns regularly to see what's working and adjust your bids and keywords accordingly," Jordan said.

Display and Video Ads: Understanding Different Ad Formats

With the basics of Google search ads covered, Jordan turned the conversation to other forms of paid advertising—**display ads** and **video ads**.

Display ads, Jordan explained, are banner-like advertisements that show up on websites within Google's display network. "These are great for **brand awareness**," he said, pulling up an example of a display ad for a clothing brand. "They're visual and tend to catch attention. You could run a display ad campaign showing off some of your best jewellery pieces."

"Would this work for generating sales, or is it just to get my name out there?" Alex asked.

"Display ads are generally better for awareness," Jordan clarified. "People might not be ready to buy right away, but they'll remember your brand the next time they're in the market for jewellery."

Next, they discussed **video ads**, which were increasingly popular on platforms like **YouTube** and **Instagram**. "If you're comfortable with video content, this could be a powerful way to showcase how your jewellery is made or show a customer wearing your pieces," Jordan said. "Video ads tend to get higher engagement, especially if they tell a story."

They emphasised that, like display ads, video ads are best for building brand awareness and engagement, but with the right targeting, they can also lead to sales.

Retargeting: Bringing Back Lost Visitors

As they dug deeper into paid advertising, Alex brought up a concern: "I'm getting a lot of visitors who browse my products but don't make a purchase. How can I bring them back?"

Jordan smiled. "That's where **retargeting** comes in."

Jordan explained that **retargeting ads** are shown to people who have already visited your website but didn't complete an action, like making a purchase. "Have you ever noticed ads for something you were browsing on one site following you around on other websites? That's retargeting in action."

Jordan walked Alex through setting up a retargeting campaign using **Google Ads** and **Facebook Ads**. "You install a **tracking pixel** on your site that tracks visitors. Then, you create ads that specifically target people who visited your site but didn't buy."

They outlined a simple strategy:

1. **Segment your audience**: Retarget visitors based on specific behaviours—like adding an item to their cart but not checking out. This is where you might offer a **discount code** or **free shipping** in the ad to encourage them to complete the purchase.

2. **Create urgency**: Jordan suggested using messaging like "Limited Stock" or "Offer Ends Soon" to nudge people

who are on the fence.

3. **Rotate ads**: "Don't show the same ad over and over," Jordan advised. "Create multiple versions to keep it fresh. If someone didn't click the first time, try a new approach."

BUDGETING AND ROI: MAXIMISING AD SPEND

Alex had one more pressing question: "How do I know if I'm spending my money wisely? I don't want to blow my budget on ads that don't work."

Jordan leaned forward, ready to explain the math behind advertising success. "This is where **ROI (Return on Investment)** comes into play. You need to measure how much you're spending on ads versus how much you're making from the traffic or sales they generate."

They broke it down with an example: "Let's say you're running a campaign with a daily budget of $10. Over a month, that's $300. If your ads generate $1,000 in sales, your ROI is over 3x, which is excellent."

To ensure their ad spend was effective, Jordan recommended tracking:

- **Cost-per-click (CPC)**: How much you're paying for each click. Ideally, you want this to be low, but remember it varies by industry and keywords.
- **Click-through rate (CTR)**: The percentage of people who see your ad and actually click on it. A high CTR means your ad is relevant and engaging.

- **Conversion rate**: The percentage of people who click on your ad and then complete a desired action (like buying a product). This is one of the most important metrics.
- **Cost-per-conversion**: How much you're spending to get someone to take that desired action. If it costs $10 in ad spend to get a sale, and you're selling products with high profit margins, that's a win.

The Highlights: Ad Strategy Essentials

Before they wrapped up, Jordan summarised the key takeaways for Alex:

1. **PPC advertising**: Start small with Google Ads, targeting specific keywords relevant to your business. Optimise your ad copy and landing pages to improve your ranking and reduce costs.
2. **Display and video ads**: These are great for building brand awareness. Use them to showcase your products in a visually engaging way, especially if you're comfortable with video content.
3. **Retargeting**: Bring back visitors who didn't buy by showing them ads that remind them of the products they viewed. Consider offering incentives like discounts or free shipping to close the sale.
4. **Track your ROI**: Make sure you're getting a good return on your ad spend by monitoring key metrics like cost-per-click, click-through rates, and conversion rates.
5. **Start with a small budget**: Test the waters with a small daily budget, and as you see results, scale your campaigns up.

TAKEAWAY FOR READERS:

For business owners like Alex, paid advertising can feel overwhelming at first, but with the right strategy, it's a powerful tool for driving traffic and sales. The key lessons from this chapter are:

1. **Start with PPC ads**: Google Ads is a great place to begin. Choose long-tail keywords that are affordable and relevant to your business.
2. **Explore different ad formats**: Display and video ads are great for raising awareness, while search ads are more direct in driving sales.
3. **Retargeting is crucial**: Retarget ads to visitors who've already shown interest but haven't converted yet.
4. **Monitor ROI**: Track your results carefully to make sure your ad spend is delivering value. Adjust your campaigns based on performance.
5. **Test and learn**: Start small, experiment with different campaigns, and scale once you know what works.

TRANSITION TO CHAPTER 7: ANALYTICS AND PERFORMANCE TRACKING

With her first paid campaigns now live, Alex felt more confident. But running ads was only half the battle—now she needed to understand the data. In the next chapter, Jordan will teach Alex how to use **analytics** to track performance, optimise campaigns, and make data-driven decisions to grow their business…

ANALYTICS AND PERFORMANCE TRACKING

ANALYSING THE DATA

A week after launching their first paid advertising campaigns, Alex found herself glued to the screen, checking the results on a loop. Clicks were coming in, but the sales still weren't matching the traffic. It felt like staring at puzzle pieces without knowing how they fit together. Frustrated, Alex called Jordan.

"Let's sit down and go through the numbers," Jordan suggested when they met later that afternoon. They settled into Alex's workshop with a laptop and a fresh cup of coffee, ready to dive into the world of **analytics**.

Jordan smiled as they opened up Google Analytics. "This is where we figure out what's working and what needs adjusting. Analytics isn't just about tracking numbers—it's about using that data to make informed decisions that move your business forward."

Introduction to Web Analytics: What to Track and Why

Jordan began by explaining the basics of **web analytics**. "Analytics helps you understand how visitors are interacting with your website. You can track where they're coming from, what they're clicking on, how long they're staying, and most importantly, why they're leaving without making a purchase."

They opened up the Google Analytics dashboard and pointed out key metrics that Alex needed to monitor regularly:

1. **Traffic sources**: "This shows where your visitors are coming from—whether it's organic search, social media, direct visits, or paid ads. It helps you see which channels are driving the most traffic."

2. **Bounce rate**: "This tells you the percentage of people who land on your site and then leave without interacting. A high bounce rate can mean your site isn't engaging, or people aren't finding what they're looking for."

3. **Session duration**: "How long are visitors staying on your site? If they're leaving after just a few seconds, it's a sign that something's off with your content or user experience."

4. **Conversion rate**: "This is one of the most important metrics. It shows how many visitors are completing a desired action, like making a purchase or signing up for your newsletter. If your conversion rate is low, you may need to optimise your landing pages."

5. **Exit pages**: "This tells you which pages people are leaving from. If a lot of visitors are dropping off at a certain point, it might indicate a problem on that page."

Alex started jotting down notes as she began to understand the importance of each metric. "So, it's not just about traffic—it's about what people do when they get to my site?"

"Exactly," Jordan confirmed. "It's better to have 100 engaged visitors who make purchases than 1,000 who bounce without buying anything."

Tools Overview: Google Analytics, Social Media Analytics, and SEO Tools

Jordan then took Alex through some of the most important **tools** they'd need to track their site's performance and their digital marketing efforts.

1. Google Analytics

"This is your main tool for tracking website performance," Jordan explained. "It gives you a full view of how visitors interact with your site, where they come from, and how they convert. You'll spend a lot of time here understanding how to optimise your pages."

Jordan highlighted a few key features:

- **Real-time data**: "You can see who's on your site right now and what they're doing."
- **Audience insights**: "Google Analytics breaks down your audience by demographics, location, and even device. If you see a lot of visitors on mobile, for example, you'll want to make sure your site is optimised for mobile."

2. Social Media Analytics

Next, they switched over to **Instagram Insights** and **Facebook Analytics**. "Every social platform has its own analytics dashboard," Jordan explained. "For Instagram, you can track things like:

- **Engagement rate**: How many people are liking, commenting, and sharing your posts.

- **Reach**: The number of unique accounts that saw your posts.
- **Impressions**: The total number of times your post was seen."

"For Facebook," Jordan continued, "you'll want to look at similar metrics—engagement, reach, and click-through rates on your posts. These will help you see which types of content are resonating with your audience."

3. SEO Tools

Finally, Jordan introduced Alex to tools like **Google Search Console** and **Ahrefs** for tracking SEO performance.

"**Google Search Console** shows how your site is performing in search results. You can track which keywords are driving traffic, see your site's ranking, and even fix technical issues like broken links or slow page speeds."

"**Ahrefs** is a paid tool, but it's incredibly powerful for tracking backlinks, keyword performance, and doing competitor analysis. You can see what keywords your competitors are ranking for and find new opportunities for your own site."

Data Interpretation: Analysing the Metrics to Make Informed Decisions

With the tools laid out, Jordan and Alex started diving into the numbers for Alex's site. "Okay, let's look at what we've got," Jordan said, pulling up the traffic report for the past month.

1. **Traffic Sources**: Jordan clicked on the report showing where Alex's visitors were coming from. "It looks like most of your traffic is coming from social media, which is great

—but your paid ads aren't driving as much traffic as we'd hoped."

Alex frowned. "What does that mean? Are the ads not working?"

"Not necessarily," Jordan replied. "Let's look at the ad performance itself." They switched over to the Google Ads dashboard and saw that the **click-through rate (CTR)** was lower than expected. "Your ads are getting impressions, but the CTR is a bit low. This means the ads might need better copy or more compelling visuals."

Jordan made a note to revise the ad copy, perhaps emphasising a limited-time offer or highlighting free shipping.

2. **Bounce Rate**: Next, they analysed the bounce rate for Alex's landing page. "Your bounce rate is a bit high, which suggests that visitors are leaving without exploring your site. Let's check the page speed and see if the content matches what people expect when they click your ads."

They ran a quick **page speed test** and found that the landing page took longer to load than expected, which could be turning visitors away. "We'll need to optimise the images and maybe check your cache settings to speed things up," Jordan suggested.

3. **Conversion Rate**: Finally, they looked at the conversion rate. "It's lower than we'd like, but that's okay for now," Jordan reassured Alex. "You're still in the testing phase, so the key is to keep improving. Let's experiment with different CTAs and offer a discount code to encourage purchases."

Setting Up Goals and Funnels in Google Analytics

Jordan then walked Alex through a more advanced feature: **setting up goals** in Google Analytics.

"Goals allow you to track specific actions on your site, like purchases, sign-ups, or even time spent on a page. You can create a goal for each of these, and Google Analytics will show you how well you're doing at getting visitors to complete those actions."

Jordan created a goal for product purchases and another for newsletter sign-ups. "Now we can track how many people are completing these actions and which traffic sources are driving those conversions."

Next, they set up a **funnel** to see where visitors were dropping off in the purchasing process. Jordan outlined a typical funnel for Alex's site:

1. Homepage visit
2. Product page visit
3. Add to cart
4. Checkout

"We can track each step of the funnel and see where visitors are getting stuck," Jordan explained. "If a lot of people are adding items to their cart but not checking out, it could mean your checkout process needs work."

A/B Testing: Optimising for Performance

With the basics of tracking in place, Jordan introduced the concept of **A/B testing**. "This is one of the best ways to optimise your website and ads. You create two versions of the same page or ad, change one element, and see which performs better."

They decided to start by testing different headlines on Alex's product pages. "You could try one headline that emphasises the uniqueness of your handmade jewellery, and another that highlights a discount or limited-time offer. After a couple of weeks, you'll see which one converts better."

Alex loved the idea. "So it's like experimenting with different approaches to see what works best?"

"Exactly," Jordan said. "It's a constant process of testing, learning, and improving."

The Highlights: Data-Driven Decision Making

As they wrapped up their session, Jordan summarised the most important points for Alex to keep in mind:

1. **Traffic sources**: Use Google Analytics to see where your traffic is coming from—social media, paid ads, or organic search—and focus on the channels that are performing best.
2. **Bounce rate and session duration**: Keep an eye on how long visitors are staying on your site and whether they're engaging with your content. A high bounce rate could signal issues with page speed or content relevance.
3. **Conversion rate**: Track the percentage of visitors who complete a purchase or sign up for your newsletter. Use this data to identify areas for improvement.
4. **Funnel tracking**: Set up goals and funnels to understand where visitors drop off in the buying process, and optimise those steps.
5. **A/B testing**: Continuously test different elements of your website and ads to see what performs best, from headlines and images to CTAs and offers.

TAKEAWAY FOR READERS:

For entrepreneurs like Alex, understanding and using analytics is the key to making informed decisions and improving online performance. The key lessons from this chapter are:

1. **Analytics is about insights**: Use tools like Google Analytics to track traffic, bounce rate, and conversion rates. This data helps you understand what's working and what isn't.
2. **Traffic sources matter**: Identify which channels (social media, paid ads, SEO) are driving the most valuable traffic to your site.
3. **Conversion rate optimisation**: Keep a close eye on conversion rates and set up goals to track the most important actions on your site, like purchases or sign-ups.
4. **A/B testing**: Experiment with different versions of pages, ads, and CTAs to see what resonates most with your audience.
5. **Continuous improvement**: Analytics isn't a one-time task—it's an ongoing process of testing, learning, and optimising.

TRANSITION TO CHAPTER 8: LEVERAGING DATA FOR STRATEGY REFINEMENT

Now that Alex understood the basics of tracking and analysing her website's performance, the next step was using that data to refine and improve her strategy. In the next chapter, Jordan would show Alex how to make **data-driven decisions**—adjusting content, SEO, and ad strategies to continuously optimise and grow their business…

LEVERAGING DATA FOR STRATEGY REFINEMENT

BACK AT THE CAFÉ FOR A STRATEGY SESSION

It was a rainy afternoon, and Alex and Jordan had decided to meet up at the same cozy café where they'd first discussed paid advertising. The café's soft lighting and the rhythmic sound of raindrops tapping against the windows provided the perfect backdrop for a deeper dive into Alex's growing pool of data. Alex sipped their coffee, feeling both excited and overwhelmed by the numbers they'd been tracking over the past few weeks.

"I've been tracking everything," Alex said, setting down their cup and opening a notebook filled with charts and notes. "I've got all this data, but I don't know how to turn it into something actionable. How do I keep improving without getting lost in all these numbers?"

Jordan nodded and pulled out his laptop, ready to guide Alex through the next phase. "That's where **data-driven decisions** come into play. We're going to use all this information to refine your strategy and create a cycle of continuous improvement."

Data-Driven Decisions: Using Analytics to Improve Your Strategy

Jordan pulled up the **Google Analytics** dashboard and started explaining the core principles of data-driven decisions.

"Think of data as your map," Jordan said. "It shows you where you're winning, where you're losing, and what you need to adjust. Let's go over how to break it down."

Step 1: Identify What's Working

The first step was to find the **top performers** in terms of content, traffic sources, and products.

Jordan clicked through the analytics reports to show Alex where to look. "Start by identifying which of your blog posts, product pages, or ads are bringing in the most traffic and conversions. Let's say one of your posts on 'How to Style Handmade Jewellery for Weddings' is driving a lot of traffic and getting shared on social media. That's a signal that your audience loves this type of content."

They highlighted some key metrics:
- **Top-performing pages**: Which blog posts, product pages, or landing pages are getting the most traffic? What's the bounce rate and session duration on these pages?
- **Conversion rate by source**: Which traffic sources (organic search, social media, paid ads) are driving the most conversions?
- **Best-selling products**: Look at sales data to identify which products are most popular.

Jordan continued, "Once you know what's working, you can double down on it. Create more content around topics that are performing well, or expand your advertising budget on channels that are driving conversions."

Step 2: Analyse What's Underperforming

Next, Jordan guided Alex through the process of identifying **what's not working**.

"Let's take a look at your exit pages," Jordan said, pulling up the report. "If a lot of visitors are leaving from your checkout page without completing a purchase, there could be a problem with the checkout process. Maybe it's too complicated, or maybe there's a hidden shipping fee that's turning people off."

Jordan recommended:

- **Check for high exit rates**: Look at which pages have high exit rates. These are the pages where visitors are leaving without taking action. It could mean the content isn't relevant, the design isn't engaging, or there's a technical issue.
- **Investigate low-performing products**: If certain products aren't selling, it might be time to tweak their descriptions, images, or even rethink your pricing.
- **Look at low-converting traffic sources**: If a lot of your social media traffic isn't converting, you may need to re-evaluate the content you're posting on those platforms or adjust your ad targeting.

"This isn't about failure," Jordan explained. "It's about using data to spot the weak points in your strategy and course-correcting before they become bigger problems."

Continuous Improvement: The Cycle of Analyse, Adapt, and Act

Jordan explained the importance of **continuous improvement**—an ongoing cycle where you analyse data, adapt your strategy, and take action based on what you've learned.

"We call this the **analyse, adapt, and act cycle**," Jordan said. "It's a method that keeps you flexible. You're always learning from your results and making small adjustments, which lead to bigger wins over time."

Step 1: Analyse

Look at your data regularly. This means diving into your analytics reports at least once a week and checking:
- Which traffic sources are bringing in the most valuable visitors?
- What content is driving engagement and conversions?
- Are there any patterns in customer behaviour (e.g., seasonal sales spikes)?

Step 2: Adapt

Use what you've learned to tweak your strategy. For example:
- **Double down** on high-performing content: If certain blog posts or products are driving a lot of traffic, create similar content or promote those products more heavily.
- **Improve low-performing pages**: If a certain product page has a high bounce rate, rewrite the product description, add better photos, or simplify the navigation.
- **Adjust your marketing budget**: Shift more budget to the platforms or ad types that are delivering the best ROI.

Step 3: Act

Finally, put your insights into action. Test your changes and monitor the results. If your tweaks work, keep refining them. If they don't, return to the data and try something else.

Jordan made it clear that this process never ends. "The more you analyse and adapt, the more efficient your strategy becomes."

Case Studies of Successful Data-Driven Strategies

Jordan knew that examples would help solidify these concepts, so they shared a few **case studies** from their experience working with other small businesses.

Case Study 1: A Local Coffee Shop's Content Strategy

Jordan explained how a local coffee shop used data to identify the types of blog posts their customers enjoyed the most.

"We found that their posts about 'Coffee Brewing Techniques' and 'Sustainability in Coffee Sourcing' were getting shared like crazy. So, we pivoted their content strategy to focus on educational content about coffee, and their organic traffic skyrocketed. They also created downloadable guides to brewing coffee at home, which boosted their email sign-ups."

Lesson: By focusing on **data-proven content**, the coffee shop was able to attract more engaged visitors and convert them into loyal customers.

Case Study 2: An Online Clothing Boutique's Product Pages

Another case Jordan shared involved an online clothing boutique that was struggling with low conversion rates. After analysing their product pages, they found that many visitors were dropping off because the product descriptions were vague, and the photos didn't show enough detail.

"We rewrote the descriptions to be more detailed, emphasising the quality of the fabrics and the fit of the clothing. We also added more product images, showing the items from multiple angles. Almost immediately, their bounce rate dropped, and their sales increased by 25%."

Lesson: **Optimising product pages** with better descriptions and images can make a huge difference in conversions.

Pitfalls to Avoid: Common Mistakes in Data-Driven Strategies

As helpful as data can be, Jordan warned Alex about a few common pitfalls that can trip up entrepreneurs:

1. Focusing on Vanity Metrics

"Don't get distracted by **vanity metrics**," Jordan cautioned. "Metrics like the number of followers or page views can be misleading if they're not translating into sales or meaningful engagement."

For example, having 10,000 Instagram followers might seem impressive, but if none of them are engaging with your content or buying your products, it's not a useful metric. Focus on what really matters: **conversions, engagement rates, and ROI**.

2. Overcomplicating the Data

Jordan encouraged Alex to avoid getting bogged down by every single data point. "It's easy to get lost in the numbers and start tracking metrics that don't really matter. Focus on the metrics that are directly tied to your goals—like conversion rates, traffic from key sources, and customer lifetime value."

3. Not Acting on Insights

"Too many businesses collect data but don't use it," Jordan said, shaking their head. "Don't fall into the trap of analysis paralysis. Once you spot a trend or problem, act on it. Even small changes can lead to big improvements."

The Highlights: Refining Your Strategy Through Data

By the end of the session, Alex felt more confident about turning data into action. Jordan summarised the key points:

1. **Data-driven decisions**: Use analytics to identify what's working and what isn't. Let the data guide your strategy, not assumptions or guesses.
2. **Analyse, adapt, act**: Follow the continuous improvement cycle—regularly check your data, adapt your approach, and take action based on the insights.
3. **Focus on meaningful metrics**: Avoid vanity metrics and prioritise data that directly impacts your business, like conversion rates and ROI.

4. **Optimise underperforming areas**: Use data to spot weak points in your strategy, whether it's a low-converting product page or a high bounce rate on your blog posts.
5. **Don't wait—take action**: Once you uncover valuable insights, act on them. Test changes, monitor the results, and keep refining.

TAKEAWAY FOR READERS:

Just like Alex, business owners can often feel overwhelmed by data, but the key is to **use that data to refine your strategy** continuously. The lessons from this chapter are:
1. **Data is your guide**: Use it to identify strengths and weaknesses in your content, products, and traffic sources.
2. **Continuous improvement**: Adopt the cycle of analysing, adapting, and acting to keep refining your digital marketing strategy.
3. **Focus on conversions**: While traffic and engagement are important, the ultimate goal is driving conversions—whether it's sales, sign-ups, or leads.
4. **Don't overcomplicate**: Track the metrics that matter most to your business goals, and don't get lost in unnecessary data.
5. **Be proactive**: When you see opportunities for improvement, act quickly. The faster you adapt, the better your results.

TRANSITION TO CHAPTER 9: SECURITY AND COMPLIANCE

With a data-driven strategy in place, Alex was beginning to see consistent growth in her online presence. But as her website expanded, new concerns emerged—how to keep her customers' data secure and comply with legal regulations. In the next chapter, Jordan would help Alex navigate the complexities of **web security** and ensure compliance with privacy laws like **GDPR, POPI** and **CCPA**...

Mike Hendrikse

SECURITY AND COMPLIANCE

ALEX'S WORKSHOP—A NEW CONCERN

It was a typical day in Alex's workshop, the familiar scent of polished metals and the hum of soft music filling the air. But today, Alex's thoughts weren't on creating new designs. As their website traffic and sales grew, so did the number of customer emails, orders, and credit card transactions flowing through their site. The excitement of growth had given way to anxiety about one key issue—**security**.

Alex was beginning to feel the weight of responsibility that came with collecting customer data. "I've been reading about all these data breaches and privacy laws," Alex said, looking up from her laptop when Jordan walked in. "It's starting to freak me out. How do I make sure my site is secure? And what's all this talk about GDPR and compliance?"

Jordan, always prepared for these moments, pulled up a chair. "You're right to be thinking about this. As your business grows, protecting your website and ensuring **legal compliance** becomes critical. Let's start with the basics of **web security** and then dive into what you need to know about **data privacy laws**."

Web Security: Protecting Your Site and Customer Data

Jordan opened up a document on his laptop, already filled with bullet points about **web security basics**. "Think of your website like a storefront. Just as you'd install a lock on your door, you need layers of protection for your site to keep hackers out and your customers' data safe."

He broke down the most important steps:

1. SSL Certificates

"The first thing you need is an **SSL certificate**. It encrypts the data that passes between your website and your customers, like their credit card information and personal details."

Jordan clicked on Alex's website and pointed to the address bar. "See how there's a padlock next to your URL? That's a sign you already have an SSL certificate. But make sure it's regularly updated, and if you ever see that padlock disappear, address it immediately. Without SSL, search engines like Google will flag your site as unsafe, and customers will lose trust."

2. Regular Backups

"You also need to back up your website regularly," Jordan continued. "In case anything goes wrong—whether it's a hack, a server failure, or even just a bad update—you'll want to restore your site quickly."

Jordan recommended using an automated backup service, ensuring that Alex had both on-site and off-site backups. "This way, even if your hosting service goes down, you'll have a copy of your site somewhere else."

3. Strong Passwords and User Management

Alex's eyes widened as Jordan emphasised the importance of strong passwords. "Use a **password manager** and make sure your passwords are long and complex. And if you have multiple people managing your site—say, developers or content creators—give them the minimum access they need. **Limit admin privileges** to only those who absolutely require them."

4. Firewalls and Security Plugins

Jordan next walked Alex through installing a **website firewall**. "A firewall acts as a gatekeeper between your site and the outside world, blocking malicious traffic."

They also suggested adding **security plugins** like **Wordfence** or **Sucuri**, which monitor suspicious activity, protect against malware, and offer additional layers of protection.

Legal Considerations: GDPR, CCPA, and Data Privacy

After covering the technical aspects of web security, Jordan turned to the legal side of things—**data privacy laws**. He knew Alex had been hearing terms like **GDPR, POPI** and **CCPA**, and now it was time to unpack what those meant for their business.

1. GDPR (General Data Protection Regulation)

Jordan pulled up an article explaining **GDPR**, the European data privacy law that governs how businesses collect, store, and use personal data from EU citizens.

"Even if your business is based outside the EU, you're still subject to **GDPR** if you're collecting data from European customers," Jordan said. "That means if you sell jewellery to someone in Germany or France, you need to follow these rules."

Jordan outlined the key GDPR principles:

- **User consent**: "You need to get explicit consent from visitors before collecting their data—this is why you see those pop-ups about accepting cookies."
- **Data access**: "Customers have the right to access the data you've collected on them. They can also ask for that data to be deleted."
- **Breach notifications**: "If there's ever a data breach, you're required to inform affected customers within 72 hours."

Alex took a deep breath. "So I need to add a cookie consent banner to my site and make sure customers can request to see or delete their data?"

"Exactly," Jordan said. "Most modern website platforms have GDPR compliance tools built in, but you'll want to double-check that everything is set up properly."

2. CCPA (California Consumer Privacy Act)

Next up was **CCPA**, a data privacy law specific to California, which had some similarities to GDPR but was tailored to U.S.-based customers.

"Even if you're not based in California, if you collect data from California residents, you're required to comply," Jordan explained. "The key with CCPA is giving customers the right to know what data you're collecting, the ability to opt out of having their data sold, and the right to request data deletion."

Jordan suggested adding a **Privacy Policy** to Alex's website that clearly explains what data is being collected, how it's used, and how customers can exercise their rights under these laws.

Certainly! Here's a paragraph on the **POPI Act** (Protection of Personal Information Act) for your South African readers to include in Chapter 9:

3. POPI Act (Protection of Personal Information Act)

In addition to GDPR and CCPA, businesses operating in South Africa need to ensure compliance with the **POPI Act** (Protection of Personal Information Act). The POPI Act is designed to protect the personal data of South African citizens, ensuring that businesses collect, store, and use this information responsibly.

Key principles of POPI include obtaining **explicit consent** from individuals before processing their data, ensuring **transparency** in how personal information is handled, and providing individuals with the right to **access**, **correct**, or **delete** their data.

Businesses must also implement appropriate security measures to safeguard personal information against unauthorised access or breaches.

Failure to comply with the POPI Act can result in significant fines or reputational damage, making it crucial for South African businesses to integrate these requirements into their data privacy practices alongside global regulations like GDPR.

Compliance Tools: Making It Easier

At this point, Alex's head was spinning with all the legalities. Jordan sensed this and reassured them. "You don't have to handle this alone. There are tools and services that can help make sure you're compliant."

They recommended tools like:

- **Cookiebot** or **OneTrust** for managing cookie consent and privacy settings.
- **Termly** for generating compliant **privacy policies**, **terms and conditions**, and **cookie consent banners**.
- Shopify or WordPress GDPR compliance plugins for making compliance easier.

"These tools help automate much of the process, ensuring that you're staying on the right side of the law without getting bogged down in the details," Jordan explained.

The Highlights: Security and Compliance Essentials

Before they wrapped up, Jordan summarised the critical points for Alex:

1. **SSL certificates**: Ensure your site has an SSL certificate to encrypt customer data and protect your site's credibility.
2. **Regular backups**: Back up your website frequently, both on-site and off-site, to protect against data loss.
3. **User management and strong passwords**: Limit access to your site's backend and use strong, complex passwords managed by a password manager.
4. **Firewalls and security plugins**: Install a website firewall and security plugins to monitor and block potential threats.
5. **GDPR and CCPA compliance**: Make sure you're following data privacy laws, particularly if you have customers from the EU or California. Use tools to automate consent management and privacy policy updates.

TAKEAWAY FOR READERS:

For business owners like Alex, understanding and implementing web security and data privacy measures is essential as their online presence grows. The key lessons from this chapter are:

1. **Web security**: Protect your site with SSL certificates, regular backups, strong passwords, and firewalls. Use security plugins to monitor potential threats.
2. **GDPR compliance**: If you collect data from EU customers, ensure you get explicit consent, offer data access and deletion, and prepare for breach notifications.
3. **CCPA compliance**: If you have California customers, give them the right to know what data you're collecting and allow them to opt out or request deletion.
4. **Use compliance tools**: Automate cookie consent, privacy policies, and user rights management with trusted tools to simplify the process.
5. **Stay proactive**: As your business grows, continue to monitor security and compliance to avoid potential risks and legal issues.

TRANSITION TO CHAPTER 10: FUTURE TRENDS AND INNOVATIONS

With her website now secure and compliant, Alex could finally breathe a little easier. But as Jordan reminded her, the digital landscape is constantly evolving. To stay ahead, she'd need to keep an eye on **emerging technologies** like AI, voice search, and even AR/VR in digital marketing.

In the next chapter, Jordan would take Alex on a journey through the **future trends and innovations** shaping the world of online business...

Mike Hendrikse

FUTURE TRENDS AND INNOVATIONS

A FUTURISTIC MARKETING CONFERENCE

A few months after securing her website and getting into the rhythm of tracking analytics, Alex found herself at her first digital marketing conference. The venue was buzzing with energy—vendors displaying cutting-edge technology, speakers discussing future trends, and entrepreneurs like Alex soaking it all in.

Alex had convinced Jordan to attend with her, and as they walked into the main hall, they could see the excitement on Jordan's face. "This is where the future of digital marketing is happening," Jordan said. "We're going to hear about technologies that will shape how you do business in the coming years. Some of it might seem far off now, but the smart businesses are already preparing."

They grabbed seats near the front of the main stage, where a panel of experts was about to discuss the next big trends in online marketing—**artificial intelligence (AI)**, **voice search**, and **augmented reality (AR)/virtual reality (VR)**.

As the lights dimmed, Alex felt a mix of curiosity and anxiety. "It feels like there's always something new to keep up with," she whispered to Jordan.

"That's the key," Jordan replied, leaning closer. "You don't have to adopt everything right away. But understanding where the market is headed will help you adapt and stay ahead of your competition."

Emerging Technologies: AI, Voice Search, and AR/VR

The first speaker began discussing **artificial intelligence (AI)** in digital marketing, and Alex leaned forward, intrigued.

1. AI in SEO and Content Creation

The speaker explained how **AI** was already changing how businesses approached **search engine optimisation (SEO)** and **content creation**. "Tools like **AI-driven keyword analysis** and **content generators** are helping businesses identify trends and optimise their content faster than ever before," the speaker said.

Jordan turned to Alex. "AI tools like **Surfer SEO** or **Frase** can help you with **on-page SEO**, identifying the best keywords to target and even suggesting content improvements. This saves you hours of manual research."

The speaker continued, showing examples of businesses using **AI-powered chatbots** for customer service. "AI chatbots can handle customer inquiries instantly, even providing personalised recommendations based on browsing history or past purchases."

Alex was fascinated but a little skeptical. "But won't customers know they're talking to a robot?"

Jordan nodded. "Yes, but it's becoming more accepted, especially if it leads to faster service. You can use AI to answer common questions, process orders, or even recommend products, freeing you up to focus on other areas of your business."

The speaker emphasised that AI could also be used for **predictive analytics**—forecasting customer behaviour based on past actions and adjusting marketing strategies accordingly.

2. Voice Search Optimisation

The next speaker dove into **voice search**, a rapidly growing area due to the rise of smart devices like **Amazon Alexa, Google Assistant**, and **Apple's Siri**. "Pretty soon nearly half of all internet searches are expected to be voice-activated," they said. "This will fundamentally change how businesses approach SEO."

Alex glanced at Jordan, wide-eyed. "So, people won't even type in search queries anymore?"

"Not always," Jordan said. "Instead of typing 'best handmade jewellery,' they'll say something like, 'What's the best place to buy custom jewellery?' Voice search queries are more conversational and longer, so optimising for **long-tail keywords** is becoming even more important."

The speaker explained how businesses needed to start **optimising for voice search** by focusing on natural language and question-based keywords. "You need to anticipate the questions your audience is asking—like 'How do I clean my handmade jewellery?'—and create content that directly answers those questions."

Jordan made a note in their phone. "This is huge for SEO. It's all about **featured snippets**, the short, direct answers that voice assistants pull from the web. If you can optimise your content for those, you're more likely to be the answer when someone asks their smart speaker for recommendations."

3. Augmented Reality (AR) and Virtual Reality (VR) in Marketing

As the conversation shifted to **AR/VR**, Alex's mind began racing with possibilities. The speaker described how **augmented real-**

ity (AR) allows customers to "try on" products digitally before making a purchase.

"Imagine a customer using their phone to see how one of your necklaces would look on them in real time," the speaker said. "That's AR in action. It brings the in-store experience into the online world."

Alex's eyes lit up. "That would be amazing for my business. It's hard for people to know how jewellery will look on them when they're shopping online."

Jordan nodded. "Exactly. Brands like Warby Parker and IKEA are already using AR to let customers try on glasses or visualise furniture in their homes. It creates an interactive shopping experience."

The speaker continued, explaining that **virtual reality** (VR) was still in its early stages for most businesses but had immense potential. "VR could let customers step into a virtual showroom where they can browse your entire collection in 3D."

Jordan leaned over to Alex. "These technologies are still developing, but keeping them on your radar is important. As AR becomes more accessible, even small businesses will be able to create virtual 'try before you buy' experiences."

Adapting to Change: Staying Ahead of Digital Trends

After the presentation, Alex and Jordan grabbed coffee at the conference café to discuss everything they'd just heard.

"This feels like a lot to take in," Alex admitted, stirring their coffee. "I don't have the resources for AI or AR right now, but I don't want to fall behind."

Jordan nodded, understanding the concern. "You don't need to adopt everything all at once. The key is to be **aware of the trends** and start small. You can experiment with AI tools for SEO and customer service, or update your content strategy to account for voice search."

Jordan pulled out his phone and began typing. "Here's what I recommend for now:

1. **Start experimenting with AI**: Use AI tools like **Surfer SEO** to help with content optimisation or chatbots to handle basic customer inquiries.
2. **Optimise for voice search**: Start integrating more natural, conversational keywords into your SEO strategy. Think about what questions your customers are asking.
3. **Keep an eye on AR developments**: Look out for affordable AR tools that could enhance your customer's shopping experience in the future. You don't need to jump in right away, but stay informed."

Alex sipped her coffee, feeling a bit more reassured. "So it's about adapting step by step?"

"Exactly," Jordan said. "Digital marketing is always evolving, but the businesses that stay flexible and experiment with new technologies are the ones that stay ahead. Keep testing, learning, and adjusting your strategy."

Predictions for the Next 5 Years: What to Expect

As they wrapped up their discussion, Jordan shared some final thoughts on what to expect in the next five years.

- **AI-driven marketing**: "In the next few years, AI will become more mainstream, automating everything from content creation to customer support. Businesses that adopt AI early will be able to scale faster and offer more personalised customer experiences."

- **The rise of voice search**: "Voice search will continue to grow, so expect SEO to shift more towards **conversational content** and **question-based search queries**. Businesses that optimise for voice will dominate search rankings."

- **AR and VR in eCommerce**: "AR will become a standard feature for online shopping experiences, especially in industries like fashion, jewellery, and home decor. Expect to see more 'virtual fitting rooms' and interactive product demos."

- **Data privacy and personalisation**: "With all this technology, consumers are becoming more conscious of their privacy. Businesses will need to strike a balance between **personalisation** and **data protection**, ensuring that customers feel secure while enjoying a tailored experience."

Jordan leaned back, smiling. "The future is exciting, and the tools that seem futuristic now will soon be accessible to businesses of all sizes."

The Highlights: Preparing for the Future

Before they left the conference, Jordan recapped the main takeaways from the session:
1. **AI**: Use AI tools for content optimisation, SEO, and customer service to automate tasks and personalise experiences.

2. **Voice search**: Optimise for conversational, question-based search queries, and aim for featured snippets to capture voice search traffic.
3. **AR/VR**: Keep an eye on AR developments to enhance online shopping experiences. AR will become increasingly important for product-based businesses.
4. **Data privacy and personalisation**: As you adopt new technologies, ensure you protect customer data while delivering a personalised experience.
5. **Adapt gradually**: You don't need to adopt every new technology at once. Start small, experiment, and adapt your strategy as these tools become more accessible.

TAKEAWAY FOR READERS:

The digital landscape is rapidly changing, and while it may seem overwhelming, staying informed and flexible is the key to success. The lessons from this chapter are:

1. **AI is here**: AI-driven tools can help with content optimisation, customer service, and predictive analytics. Start experimenting to save time and personalise your customer experience.
2. **Voice search is growing**: Optimise for voice search by focusing on natural, conversational keywords and aiming for featured snippets.
3. **AR and VR are the future of eCommerce**: Augmented reality will transform how customers interact with products online. Keep an eye on AR tools to enhance the shopping experience.

4. **Balance technology with data privacy**: As you adopt these innovations, ensure you maintain customer trust by protecting their data and offering transparency.
5. **Stay adaptable**: The businesses that thrive are the ones that are open to experimenting with new tools and trends, while continually refining their strategies.

TRANSITION TO CHAPTER 11: CASE STUDIES AND EXAMPLES

As Alex left the conference, her mind was buzzing with ideas about the future. But they also wanted to see how other businesses had successfully navigated these changes. In the next chapter, Jordan would walk Alex through real-world **case studies**, showcasing companies that had implemented these strategies effectively—and the lessons they could learn from their successes and mistakes…

CASE STUDIES AND EXAMPLES

A QUIET AFTERNOON IN THE WORKSHOP

Back in the familiar surroundings of Alex's workshop, the flurry of the digital marketing conference was starting to settle into actionable insights. While Alex was excited about the future trends she had learned about, she couldn't shake the feeling that they needed to see how these strategies played out in the real world before diving in too deeply.

That's when Jordan stopped by with a folder full of **case studies**—examples of businesses that had successfully navigated the same challenges Alex was facing. As they settled in with a cup of tea, Alex asked, "I get the theory, but what does it look like when companies actually put these strategies into practice?"

Jordan smiled and opened the folder. "I figured you'd say that. Let me show you a few stories that might resonate with what you're doing. We'll look at some success stories, but I'll also show you examples of businesses that made mistakes and how they corrected them."

Case Study 1: Success in Scaling with SEO and Content Marketing

Company: A small, family-owned business selling handcrafted home décor.

Challenge: Much like Alex's jewellery business, they were struggling to scale beyond local customers and had very little organic traffic to their website. They knew they needed to leverage **content marketing** and **SEO** but didn't know where to start.

Solution: They began by focusing on creating content that was highly relevant to their target audience. Instead of generic blog posts, they produced:
- **How-to guides** (e.g., "How to Style a Rustic Farmhouse Living Room")
- **Product care tutorials** (e.g., "Caring for Your Handcrafted Wooden Furniture")
- **Seasonal décor tips** (e.g., "Fall Decorating Ideas with Handmade Wooden Pieces")

Using tools like **Google Keyword Planner**, they optimised their content for long-tail keywords that their customers were searching for, such as "handmade wooden farmhouse décor" and "custom wood signs for weddings." They also worked on **backlinking** by reaching out to interior design blogs and collaborating with influencers who were passionate about rustic décor.

Results:
- In 12 months, their **organic traffic** increased by 200%.
- They saw a 50% growth in sales from online customers, most of whom had found them through search engines.
- Their blog posts and guides were shared widely on **Pinterest**, driving additional traffic.

Lesson for Alex: By focusing on **highly relevant content** that solved customer problems and optimising it for **SEO**, the business was able to attract new customers from across the country. For Alex, this could mean creating similar blog posts or videos—"How to Style Custom Jewellery for Special Events" or "The Best Ways to Care for Handmade Jewellery"—and making sure the content is **SEO-friendly**.

Case Study 2: A Jewellery Brand's Social Media Transformation

Company: An online-only jewellery retailer specialising in minimalist pieces.

Challenge: This brand had built a decent following on Instagram but wasn't seeing much engagement or sales. Their posts felt "random," with no clear strategy behind them. They were also hesitant to invest in **paid social media ads** because they weren't sure if it would deliver results.

Solution: They started by focusing on **content consistency** and creating posts that reflected their brand story. They established a clear **content calendar**, ensuring that their feed alternated between:

- High-quality product photos
- Customer testimonials (user-generated content)
- Behind-the-scenes videos showing the design and creation process
- Style guides for different occasions (e.g., "How to Wear Minimalist Jewellery to a Wedding")

They also began experimenting with **Instagram and Facebook ads**. Instead of promoting their entire product range, they ran **targeted campaigns** around specific collections—using audience targeting tools to reach people who had previously visited their website or engaged with their Instagram page.

Results:

- Engagement on their Instagram posts doubled within six months, and their follower count grew by 30%.
- **Retargeting ads** resulted in a 40% increase in abandoned cart recovery, helping them convert visitors who hadn't initially made a purchase.

- Their video content, especially behind-the-scenes stories, led to a surge in followers and engagement as customers connected more personally with the brand.

Lesson for Alex: A **consistent social media strategy**, focused on engaging and educational content, can help build brand loyalty and drive sales. Retargeting ads are especially powerful for bringing back visitors who may have shown interest but didn't buy right away. Alex could apply this by promoting specific jewellery collections and experimenting with retargeting ads to recover abandoned carts.

Case Study 3: Mistakes Made in Paid Advertising and How They Recovered

Company: A boutique clothing store transitioning from brick-and-mortar to eCommerce.

Challenge: This business decided to invest heavily in **Google Ads** but quickly ran into trouble. They chose high-competition keywords like "women's clothing" and "boutique dresses," which resulted in expensive clicks but very few sales. They had spent thousands in ad budget with almost no return on investment.

What Went Wrong:
- They had focused on **broad, high-competition keywords** instead of targeting **niche, long-tail keywords** that better fit their unique product offerings.
- Their landing pages didn't match the keywords they were bidding on. For example, customers who clicked on ads for "summer dresses" were taken to a generic product page rather than a dedicated landing page featuring their summer collection.

Solution: After realising their mistake, they pivoted by:

- Shifting their focus to more **specific, lower-competition keywords**, such as "handmade summer dresses" or "ethically sourced cotton clothing."
- Creating **dedicated landing pages** for their ad campaigns, ensuring that the content matched the user's search intent (e.g., a page for "ethical clothing" with product descriptions emphasising sustainability).
- Using **negative keywords** to filter out irrelevant searches that were eating up their ad budget.

Results:
- Within three months, they reduced their cost per click by 40% and doubled their conversion rate.
- Their ads started driving qualified traffic, resulting in a steady increase in sales and a much-improved **return on ad spend (ROAS)**.

Lesson for Alex: Paid advertising can be a powerful tool, but it's easy to burn through a budget without proper targeting and optimisation. Focus on **niche keywords** that are relevant to your products, and ensure that your ads lead customers to **specific landing pages** that match their search intent. For Alex, this might mean targeting keywords like "custom gold necklaces" or "handmade jewellery for weddings" and creating landing pages tailored to those keywords.

Case Study 4: A Retailer's Misstep in Data Privacy Compliance

Company: A growing eCommerce retailer with a wide customer base in both the U.S. and Europe.

Challenge: This retailer was growing quickly but had failed to properly implement **GDPR compliance** when they started collecting customer data from European customers. They didn't have a proper cookie consent banner, and their privacy policy wasn't transparent about how they were using customer data.

What Went Wrong:
- The business received several complaints from EU customers about unclear data practices. Eventually, they were hit with a **GDPR violation** fine, which, though not crippling, was enough to cause significant concern and damage their reputation.

Solution:
- They worked with a legal consultant to overhaul their **privacy policy** and ensure it was clear about what data they were collecting, why they were collecting it, and how customers could request access or deletion of their data.
- They implemented a proper **cookie consent banner** on their website that complied with GDPR regulations.
- They introduced a **data management system** that allowed customers to easily opt-out of data tracking or request that their personal data be deleted from the retailer's database.

Results:
- The business avoided further legal trouble and saw improved customer trust. After updating their privacy practices, they received fewer complaints, and customer satisfaction scores improved.
- They also used the opportunity to promote transparency in their marketing, showcasing their commitment to customer privacy, which resonated with privacy-conscious shoppers.

Lesson for Alex: Compliance with data privacy laws like **GDPR, POPI** and **CCPA** is critical, especially as your business grows. It's better to address these issues early to avoid legal troubles and maintain customer trust. Alex can learn from this by ensuring their site is fully compliant with privacy regulations, offering transparency in how data is collected and used.

Common Mistakes and How to Avoid Them

After reviewing the case studies, Jordan summed up a few **common mistakes** that businesses often make—and how Alex could avoid them:

1. **Ignoring Data**: Many businesses collect data but don't act on it. "Use your analytics tools to track what's working and what isn't. If a blog post or product page isn't performing, don't wait—adjust it right away."

2. **Broad Keyword Targeting**: Overly broad keywords in paid advertising can lead to high costs with little return. "Focus on niche, long-tail keywords that are specific to your products."

3. **Inconsistent Social Media Content**: Posting without a clear strategy or consistent schedule often leads to disengagement. "Use an editorial calendar and plan content that reflects your brand and resonates with your audience."

4. **Non-Optimised Landing Pages**: Sending paid traffic to a generic page instead of a targeted landing page is a missed opportunity. "Make sure your landing pages match the keywords you're targeting."

5. **Neglecting Compliance**: Data privacy issues can seriously damage your business. "Address compliance issues like

GDPR, POPI and CCPA from the from the start to avoid fines and lost trust."

TAKEAWAY FOR READERS:

Through real-world examples, it's clear that businesses of all sizes face similar challenges as they grow. The lessons from this chapter are:

1. **Targeted content and SEO**: High-quality, relevant content optimised for SEO can significantly increase traffic and sales.
2. **Consistent social media strategy**: A well-planned, consistent social media strategy, combined with targeted ads, can build engagement and drive conversions.
3. **Niche keyword focus**: In paid advertising, focus on niche keywords and create targeted landing pages to improve ROI.
4. **Privacy compliance**: Ensure your site complies with data privacy laws like GDPR, POPI and CCPA from the start to avoid fines and build customer trust.
5. **Learn from mistakes**: It's natural to make mistakes in digital marketing, but the key is to learn from them quickly and make adjustments.

TRANSITION TO CHAPTER 12: CONCLUSION AND NEXT STEPS

After reviewing these case studies, Alex felt empowered to apply what she had learned. But the journey wasn't over yet. With all the strategies now in place, it was time to think about the bigger picture—how to take everything she'd learned and create a sustainable, long-term action plan for her business. In the next and final chapter, Jordan and Alex would outline the **next steps** to implement and grow, with resources for continued learning and tools to stay ahead...

Mike Hendrikse

.

CONCLUSION AND NEXT STEPS

REFLECTING ON THE JOURNEY AT THE WORKSHOP

It had been a long, transformative journey for Alex. From the early days of feeling overwhelmed by the technicalities of building a website to now navigating advanced topics like data-driven strategy, security, and future trends, she had come a long way. As she sat in the workshop, surrounded by the tools and materials that were once the sole focus of her business, Alex realised just how much she'd learned.

Jordan was with her, of course, as they reviewed all the steps they had taken. "So, where do we go from here?" Alex asked. "I feel like I have all the pieces, but I want to make sure I don't lose momentum."

Jordan smiled, already anticipating the question. "That's exactly what today is about. We're going to create a clear **action plan** for the next few months, so you can keep building on everything you've learned. Plus, I'll share some resources and tools to help you continue growing even after we finish."

Action Plan: Implementing What You've Learned

Jordan pulled out a notepad and started sketching out a simple roadmap for Alex's next steps. They broke it down into actionable categories, each tied to specific goals and timelines.

1. Website Optimisation and SEO

- Regular SEO Audits: Set a monthly schedule to run SEO audits using tools like Google Search Console and SEMrush. "This will help you stay on top of any technical issues, track keyword rankings, and adjust your content strategy based on what's working."

- Content Updates: Every month, review your top-performing blog posts and landing pages. "Refresh them with new information, add updated keywords, and continue optimising for voice search," Jordan advised. "This keeps your content relevant and improves your search rankings."

- A/B Testing: Use A/B testing on key product pages and landing pages to refine your calls-to-action, product descriptions, and headlines. "Small changes can lead to big improvements in conversion rates," Jordan reminded Alex.

2. Social Media Strategy

- **Content Calendar**: Create a **90-day content calendar** for social media. Plan out your posts ahead of time, alternating between product showcases, behind-the-scenes content, and user-generated posts. "This keeps your social media presence active and consistent," Jordan said.

- **Ad Campaigns**: Run small, targeted **Instagram and Facebook ad campaigns** each month. "Experiment with different ad formats—carousel ads, video ads, and retargeting ads—and track the performance of each," Jordan suggested.

- **Engagement Strategy**: Dedicate time every day to interact with your followers. Respond to comments, share user-generated content, and engage with similar accounts in your niche. "Building a community takes time, but it's crucial for long-term growth."

3. Data-Driven Decision Making

- Monthly Analytics Review: Every month, block out time to review your Google Analytics, social media insights, and ad performance. "This will help you identify trends, spot underperforming areas, and adapt your strategy," Jordan explained.

- Adjust Based on Data: Based on what the analytics reveal, continuously tweak your marketing efforts. "If one traffic source is outperforming the others, shift more resources there. If a product isn't selling, rethink the way you're marketing it."

4. Security and Compliance

- **Regular Security Checks**: Set up automated security scans using tools like **Wordfence** or **Sucuri** to monitor your site for vulnerabilities. "Check your SSL certificate and backups regularly to make sure everything is in place," Jordan reminded Alex.

- **GDPR/POPI/CCPA Audits**: Once a quarter, review your **GDPR, POPI** and **CCPA** compliance practices. "Make sure your privacy policy is up to date, your cookie consent banner is working properly, and that you're offering customers an easy way to manage their data."

5. Adapting to Future Trends
   - **Experiment with AI Tools**: Over the next few months, start experimenting with **AI-driven tools** for SEO, customer service, and content creation. "Even small steps—like implementing a chatbot or using AI for keyword research—can save time and enhance customer experiences."

   - **Stay Informed**: Commit to staying ahead of the curve by following industry blogs, attending webinars, and subscribing to newsletters that cover **emerging technologies** like AI, voice search, and AR/VR.

Resources: Tools and Learning for Continued Growth
Jordan then pulled out a list of **resources and tools** to help Alex on their continued journey.
1. Learning Platforms and Courses
   - **The Online Marketer**: Offers courses and workshops on Content Creation, Prompt Engineering, SEO and social media marketing.
   - **Google Digital Garage**: A free platform with courses on digital marketing, data analytics, and online advertising.

- **Udemy**: A wide range of paid and free courses on topics like AI in marketing, voice search optimisation, and AR/VR for eCommerce.

"Continuing your education is key," Jordan explained. "The more you learn, the better you'll be able to adapt to changes in the digital landscape."

2. SEO and Analytics Tools

- **Google Search Console**: A free tool for tracking your site's performance in search, identifying SEO issues, and monitoring keyword rankings.
- **SEMrush**: A premium tool for keyword research, backlink analysis, and competitive insights.
- **Ahrefs**: Another powerful SEO tool for tracking keywords, analysing backlinks, and discovering content opportunities.

"These tools will help you stay on top of your SEO and analytics," Jordan said. "You don't have to use all of them, but pick one or two and master them."

3. Social Media Tools

- **Hootsuite** or **Buffer**: For scheduling and managing social media posts across platforms.
- **Canva or Polotno**: Free design tools for creating professional-looking social media graphics, even if you don't have a design background.
- **Facebook Ads Manager**: A powerful tool for setting up, managing, and tracking your ad campaigns.

"Tools like these make it easier to stay consistent with your social media strategy and ads," Jordan noted.

4. Security and Compliance Tools

- **Wordfence** or **Sucuri**: For monitoring your website's security and protecting against malware and hacking attempts.
- **Cookiebot**: A tool to ensure your website complies with **GDPR** and **CCPA** by managing cookie consent and user data requests.
- **Termly**: For generating compliant privacy policies, terms and conditions, and cookie banners.

"These tools will help keep your site secure and ensure that you're compliant with data privacy laws," Jordan explained.

Final Words of Advice: Embrace Continuous Learning

As they finished up the action plan, Alex took a deep breath, feeling both excited and a little nervous about everything that lay ahead. "It feels like there's still so much to learn and do."

Jordan smiled reassuringly. "There always will be. But remember, you don't need to implement everything at once. The key is to keep learning, keep testing, and keep adapting. The digital landscape will always change, but if you stay flexible and open to experimenting, you'll be able to navigate those changes successfully."

They stood up to leave, but before walking out, Jordan left Alex with one final piece of advice. "Always focus on what's most important—your customers. As long as you keep their needs at the center of everything you do, you'll continue to grow. And don't forget to celebrate your wins along the way."

Alex smiled, feeling more confident and prepared than ever. She had a clear plan, the right tools, and most importantly, the mindset to continue evolving and succeeding in the digital world.

Taking the Next Step Forward

This journey has been about more than just building a website or running ads. It's about understanding the ever-evolving digital landscape, applying strategic thinking, and staying adaptable. For Alex, and for anyone following a similar path, the key takeaway is this: **Success in the digital age requires a balance of learning, experimenting, and continuously improving.**

By following the lessons in this guide—whether it's optimising for SEO, running effective social media campaigns, securing your website, or adapting to future trends—you can create a strong online presence that not only grows your business but also builds a lasting connection with your customers.

The future of digital marketing is bright, and with the right strategies in place, you can navigate it confidently and successfully.

Next Steps and Resources

For readers who are ready to implement what they've learned, here's a **final action plan** and a **list of resources** to help you continue your journey:

Action Plan

1. **Website Optimisation**: Run regular SEO audits, update content, and A/B test landing pages.
2. **Social Media Strategy**: Create a content calendar, run small ad campaigns, and engage consistently.
3. **Data-Driven Decisions**: Review your analytics monthly and adjust your marketing based on the data.
4. **Security and Compliance**: Perform regular security checks and ensure GDPR/CCPA compliance.

5. **Experiment with New Trends**: Start experimenting with AI, optimise for voice search, and keep an eye on AR/VR developments.

Recommended Tools

- **SEO**: Google Search Console, SEMrush, Ahrefs
- **Social Media**: Hootsuite, Canva, Facebook Ads Manager
- **Security**: Wordfence, Sucuri, Cookiebot
- **Learning**: The Online Marketer, Google Digital Garage, Udemy

Further Reading

- "SEO 2024: Learn Search Engine Optimization with Smart Internet Marketing Strategies" by Adam Clarke
- "The Art of Social Media: Power Tips for Power Users" by Guy Kawasaki
- "Jab, Jab, Jab, Right Hook: How to Tell Your Story in a Noisy Social World" by Gary Vaynerchuk

I love hearing form my readers!
For questions, comments or help
with your online presence visit
THEONLINEMARKETER.AGENCY

www.ingramcontent.com/pod-product-compliance
Lightning Source LLC
Chambersburg PA
CBHW071101240526
45471CB00016B/2288